Love, Joy, Peace

I0164156

Lawson Hanson

Copyright (C) 2025 Lawson Hanson

All rights reserved.

ISBN: 9781764057851

Note: Unless otherwise specified, the cited Bible text references are extracts from the KJV (King James Version, circa 1611) with updated, more modern spelling.

Contents

Chapter 1

Best Behaviour

In the Bible book of Galatians we read about nine delightful behavioural characteristics called the *"fruit of the Spirit:"*

> 22. *But the fruit of the Spirit is love, joy, peace, longsuffering, gentleness, goodness, faith,*
> 23. *Meekness, temperance: against such there is no law.*
> — Galatians 5:22–23

The first three of these is what prompted me to use *"Love, Joy, Peace"* as the title for this book.

These best behaviour qualities become part of our new persona when we receive what Jesus called *"the promise of the Father."* We will talk about that before long.

The first fruit — *"love"* — is the Love of God from a Greek word 'agape'.

People might call this 'charity' where we give of ourself expecting nothing in return — although this is more than giving to the poor because it applies to everyone we meet.

Consider these verses:

3. And though I bestow all my goods to feed the poor, and though I give my body to be burned, and have not charity, it profiteth me nothing.

4. Charity suffereth long, and is kind; charity envieth not; charity vaunteth not itself, is not puffed up,

5. Doth not behave itself unseemly, seeketh not her own, is not easily provoked, thinketh no evil;

6. Rejoiceth not in iniquity, but rejoiceth in the truth;

7. Beareth all things, believeth all things, hopeth all things, endureth all things.

— 1 Corinthians 13:3–7

The word '*charity*' in verse 3 is translated from the same Greek word '*agape*' that got rendered as '*love*' in Galatians chapter 5 verse 22.

Paul the apostle expounds the meaning of this word — '*agape*' — '*charity*' or God's '*love*' for us.

The love we express toward each other must include patience and kindness. On our part there should be no envy and no big headed showing off.

We need to be well behaved thinking nothing but good for the other person or persons. The love we demonstrate is not for our own benefit. To the contrary it is always rejoicing in the truth of God.

Love is never conditional upon the other party's behaviour. Despite the outcome we always hope and believe for the best of results.

It's *not* man's idea of love where people give no more than they get.

Look at those eight other fruit:

Joy — *cheerfulness, calm delight*

Peace — *concord, quietness, rest*
Longsuffering — *enduring patience*
Gentleness — *nonviolence, restraint, serenity*
Goodness — *courtesy, decency, virtue*
Faith — *conviction of the truth of God*
Meekness — *humility, unassuming, unselfish*
Temperance — *evenness, impartiality, justice*

I delight in that last clause in verse 23 — *"against such there is no law."*

We should make up our mind to use these behaviours as often as we can. That should help keep us out of trouble.

Casting our eyes around the world news these days there appears to be an extreme short supply of all nine of these in most locations — sad to say.

These improvements in our conduct and demeanor and manners is one of the added bonuses given on top of the real benefit of receiving God's gift.

In Romans we get told this:

> 23. *For the wages of sin is death; but the gift of God is eternal life through Jesus Christ our Lord.*
> — Romans 6:23

Contemplate the wonder and the scope of the meaning of eternal life with God and with Jesus Christ. What a magnificent gift.

Now where did Jesus mention this *"promise"* from the heavenly *"Father?"*

In the last chapter of the gospel of Luke we read a report in which Jesus says *"I send the promise of my Father upon you"* when He spoke to the apostles after He had risen from the dead:

3

44. *And he said unto them, These are the words*
which I spake unto you, while I was yet with you,
that all things must be fulfilled, which were written
in the law of Moses, and in the prophets, and in
the psalms, concerning me.
45. *Then opened he their understanding, that they*
might understand the scriptures,
46. *And said unto them, Thus it is written, and*
thus it behoved Christ to suffer, and to rise from
the dead the third day:
47. *And that repentance and remission of sins*
should be preached in his name among all nations,
beginning at Jerusalem.
48. *And ye are witnesses of these things.*
49. *And, behold, I send the promise of my Father*
upon you: but tarry ye in the city of Jerusalem,
until ye be endued with power from on high.
50. *And he led them out as far as to Bethany, and*
he lifted up his hands, and blessed them.
51. *And it came to pass, while he blessed them, he*
was parted from them, and carried up into heaven.
— Luke 24:44–51

Again it's Luke, the writer of the book of Acts who
commences his records with these important points from
their last 40 days of interaction with the risen Jesus Christ:

1. *The former treatise have I made, O Theophilus,*
of all that Jesus began both to do and teach,
2. *Until the day in which he was taken up,*
after that he through the Holy Ghost had given
commandments unto the apostles whom he had
chosen:
3. *To whom also he shewed himself alive after*
his passion by many infallible proofs, being seen
of them forty days, and speaking of the things
pertaining to the kingdom of God:

*4. And, being assembled together with them,
commanded them that they should not depart from
Jerusalem, but wait for the promise of the Father,
which, saith he, ye have heard of me.
5. For John truly baptized with water; but ye shall
be baptized with the Holy Ghost not many days
hence.*
— Acts 1:1–5

In verse 4 Jesus commanded His apostles and disciples to
wait in Jerusalem for this miraculous gift from God.

Three verses further on we read:

*8. But ye shall receive power, after that the Holy
Ghost is come upon you: and ye shall be witnesses
unto me both in Jerusalem, and in all Judaea, and
in Samaria, and unto the uttermost part of the
earth.
9. And when he had spoken these things, while
they beheld, he was taken up; and a cloud received
him out of their sight.*
— Acts 1:8–9

This parting information is vital. His last minute
instructions. Listen up. These must not get missed.

The apostles and disciples were faithful and obedient. They
did wait as instructed. Here is the miraculous result:

*1. And when the day of Pentecost was fully come,
they were all with one accord in one place.
2. And suddenly there came a sound from heaven
as of a rushing mighty wind, and it filled all the
house where they were sitting.
3. And there appeared unto them cloven tongues
like as of fire, and it sat upon each of them.*

4. *And they were all filled with the Holy Ghost,
and began to speak with other tongues, as the
Spirit gave them utterance.*
— Acts 2:1–4

On this day of Pentecost *they were all filled with the Holy
Ghost, and began to speak with other tongues, as the Spirit
gave them utterance.*

When news of this got spread around Jerusalem a crowd of
people gathered and asked *"What meaneth this?"*

Peter the apostle who was well acquainted with the words of
their ancient prophets stood up and said:

16. *But this is that which was spoken by the
prophet Joel;*
17. *And it shall come to pass in the last days,
saith God, I will pour out of my Spirit upon all
flesh: and your sons and your daughters shall
prophesy, and your young men shall see visions,
and your old men shall dream dreams:*
18. *And on my servants and on my handmaidens
I will pour out in those days of my Spirit; and
they shall prophesy:*
19. *And I will shew wonders in heaven above, and
signs in the earth beneath; blood, and fire, and
vapour of smoke:*
20. *The sun shall be turned into darkness, and the
moon into blood, before the great and notable day
of the Lord come:*
21. *And it shall come to pass, that whosoever shall
call on the name of the Lord shall be saved.*
— Acts 2:16–21

He spoke to them at length and went on to say:

*36. Therefore let all the house of Israel know
assuredly, that God hath made the same Jesus,
whom ye have crucified, both Lord and Christ.
37. Now when they heard this, they were pricked
in their heart, and said unto Peter and to the rest
of the apostles, Men and brethren, what shall we
do?
38. Then Peter said unto them, Repent, and be
baptized every one of you in the name of Jesus
Christ for the remission of sins, and ye shall
receive the gift of the Holy Ghost.
39. For the promise is unto you, and to your
children, and to all that are afar off, even as
many as the LORD our God shall call.*
— Acts 2:36–39

Peter's instructions in verse 38 worked to perfection. Two
verses further on we read:

*41. Then they that gladly received his word were
baptized: and the same day there were added unto
them about three thousand souls.*
— Acts 2:41

Over 3,000 people experienced what Jesus called *"the promise
of the Father"* on that day. Each one of them receiving the
Holy Ghost with the audible evidence of speaking in other
tongues.

Peter's instructions in verse 38 have stood the test of time.

Since then, this experience has been available to anyone who
will call out to God, on His terms — truly *"repentant"* and in
obedience, getting *"baptised"* — *"in the name of Jesus Christ
for the remission of sins."*

I know this for certain because this is my experience too.

In my early twenties I was drinking like an alcoholic and I was a chain smoker of over 30 cigarettes each day. I was selfish, self centred and lived from one pay day to the next. Bordering on being a waste of space.

If you had asked me about my future I would have surmised that I expected to be dead by the time I reached twenty five.

I count myself most fortunate to have met a person who shared vital information that has turned out to be the real and satisfying answer for the rest of my life.

When I did reach the age of 25 years I met a student who was completing his Ph.D work at the University of Melbourne and he told me about his own life changing experience.

He told me about his miracle working God. People at his church had their needs met and got healed from sickness all the time by the power of faith in Almighty God through the action of their prayers.

He told me Jesus preached that we *"must be born again."*

See John chapter 3, verses 1 to 7 for the context.

What does *"born again"* mean?

This is the experience we read about in Acts, chapter 2.

Martin, the Ph.D student talked about the change in his own life when he received this identical experience.

"What — filled with the Holy Ghost and speaking in other tongues?"

"Yes" he assured me. *"This still happens today."*

How did that come about?

He explained that he followed the advice given to the crowd of people who gathered to find out what was happening when that initial event took place about 2,000 years ago.

Martin told me he had followed the instructions given in Acts chapter 2, verse 38 and found this to be both evidential and true:

> *"Repent, and be baptized every one of you in the name of Jesus Christ for the remission of sins, and ye shall receive the gift of the Holy Ghost."*

It took me about five or six months to accept one of his invitations to attend a meeting at the church he went to. I am so glad I did.

It felt as if I was coming home! It's a happy place with a sea of genuine smiling faces. This church has centres scattered across the world. Australia, New Zealand, Papua New Guinea, Fiji, Africa, Italy, England, Poland, Canada and more. You can find out much more at this link:

https://www.revivalcentres.org

I got baptized in water after my second meeting.

For the first time in over a decade I felt as if I had taken a step in the right direction — towards God instead of always moving the other way.

A further five weeks after I got baptized, in the manner that John the Baptist used, through a complete immersion in water, I received my own *"day of Pentecost"* experience.

It took those five weeks for me to sort out my thinking and to understand what my repentance meant. It needs a complete change of mind — I was a bit slow.

The word *"Repent"* that Peter used gets derived from the Greek word *"metanoeo"* a term that more nearly means *"to think differently"* or *"to have another mind"* or to *"reconsider"* — what we think we know.

The prefix *"meta"* means *"with change."*

Peter's exhortation to us is for the need to pause, take a step back, and allow ourselves to have a *"change in the way that we have been thinking."*

I kept on attending meetings at this church and listening to excellent talks given straight from the pages of the Bible.

One morning I was praying in a quiet voice at home. I was thanking God for the delightful and miraculous changes He had helped to bring about in my life in a matter of weeks.

Through simple prayers offered for me or by me I had stopped smoking, stopped drinking alcohol and had a longstanding pain in my nose healed. Each of those happened in an instant or over night.

My sense of taste and smell returned to normal soon after I stopped smoking — how wonderful. The next fresh tomato I tasted was sheer bliss. Another thing I noticed was my speech contained no more expletives.

As I was praying there came a change when I received the gift of the Holy Spirit. I was speaking in other tongues as the Spirit gave me the utterance. My speech was quiet and clear, yet no longer in my natural tongue.

New words streamed out from my mouth at my normal speech speed. There was no extraordinary effort required.

I could stop the praying in tongues and I could start praying in tongues again. I was in complete control of this wonderful gift that God had graciously bestowed upon me.

It felt wonderful and I kept praying for a little while longer listening to those unknown words. A verse of scripture I had heard three or four days earlier came to mind:

> 14. *For if I pray in an unknown tongue, my spirit prayeth, but my understanding is unfruitful.*

— 1 Corinthians 14:14

I realised that I was able to do what God wants:

> 24. *God is a Spirit: and they that worship him*
> *must worship him in spirit and in truth.*
> — John 4:24

I realised that miracles still *do* happen today. The God of all creation has never changed.

The Old Testament declares this:

> 6. *For I am the LORD, I change not;*
> — Malachi 3:6

The New Testament declares:

> 8. *Jesus Christ the same yesterday, and to day,*
> *and for ever.*
> — Hebrews 13:8

These promises in God's Word mean that when people receive God's promised gift of the Holy Ghost today, they will have the same experience that I had. This is the *same* experience that more than 3,000 people had on the day of Pentecost, about 2,000 years ago.

It's an unmistakable gift from God. There's no way we can fake it. God provides the words for us to speak to Him.

In an instant of time, on the 27th July, 1975, I knew for certain that God is real and that He loves me more than I can imagine. There's One God who *can* answer our call. He promises He will answer and He honours His Word.

His audible gift gives us a personal prayer language that gets used for our direct communication with Almighty God. It's a precious gift that He expects us to use every day. It brings great benefits including peace and comfort and joy. It provides Spiritual insight into the kingdom of God.

This gift called *"the promise of the Father"* has filled me with an everlasting and overflowing satisfaction originating from the True and Living God of Creation.

As I write these words in 2025 this experience has never left me and the truth and veracity of God's Word — the Bible — becomes more precious every day.

I believe in God with all my heart and mind and soul and I get to communicate with Him at every moment of every day.

The Spirit of the Living God now resides within my being — dwelling with me and walking with me — there's no more uncertainty.

If you have never experienced this miraculous spiritual rebirth — please test Peter's words for yourself.

Chapter 2

Worst Behaviour

As we look around the world today through the eyes of nightly news broadcasts we observe the increase of atrocity, calamity, corruption, despair, destruction, hatred, inhumanity, mindlessness, ruthlessness, savagery, terrorism, vandalism, violence, and we see multiple wars.

What is the matter with us? Can we not see that behaviour such as this goes against everything that God wants from us?

God is well aware that mankind continues to grow desperately wicked:

> 9. *The heart is deceitful above all things, and desperately wicked: who can know it?*
> 10. *I the LORD search the heart, I try the reins, even to give every man according to his ways, and according to the fruit of his doings.*
> — Jeremiah 17:9–10

Here is how the Psalmist describes those who have no fear or respect for Almighty God:

> 1. *The transgression of the wicked saith within my heart, that there is no fear of God before his eyes.*

2. For he flattereth himself in his own eyes, until his iniquity be found to be hateful.
3. The words of his mouth are iniquity and deceit: he hath left off to be wise, and to do good.
4. He deviseth mischief upon his bed; he setteth himself in a way that is not good; he abhorreth not evil.
— Psalms 36:1–4

Here is what God says to the wicked:

16. But unto the wicked God saith, What hast thou to do to declare my statutes, or that thou shouldest take my covenant in thy mouth?
17. Seeing thou hatest instruction, and casteth my words behind thee.
18. When thou sawest a thief, then thou consentedst with him, and hast been partaker with adulterers.
19. Thou givest thy mouth to evil, and thy tongue frameth deceit.
20. Thou sittest and speakest against thy brother; thou slanderest thine own mother's son.
21. These things hast thou done, and I kept silence; thou thoughtest that I was altogether such an one as thyself: but I will reprove thee, and set them in order before thine eyes.
22. Now consider this, ye that forget God, lest I tear you in pieces, and there be none to deliver.
— Psalms 50:16–22

Their time for correction and reproof will come.

Thinking of family and friends and acquaintances — nobody likes to be forgotten.

God is no different. He does not appreciate us when we forget about Him.

How often should we think of God? How often should we talk to God?

Given that the Living God of all Creation becomes our heavenly Father — how often should we sit down and have a good chat?

I think the answer is — at least — every day.

He is there for us to speak to at all times.

We do not want to be numbered among '*the wicked*'.

We want to be among those who love God's instruction.

We do not want to be any part of evil or wrong doing.

The next verses from the book of Galatians *precede* those we have already seen, that described the miraculous "*fruit of God's Holy Spirit.*"

These following verses outline a list of the worst of behaviours we need to *leave behind* us and never consider doing again:

> 19. *Now the works of the flesh are manifest, which are these; Adultery, fornication, uncleanness, lasciviousness,*
> 20. *Idolatry, witchcraft, hatred, variance, emulations, wrath, strife, seditions, heresies,*
> 21. *Envyings, murders, drunkenness, revellings, and such like: of the which I tell you before, as I have also told you in time past, that they which do such things shall not inherit the kingdom of God.*
> — Galatians 5:19–21

The Word of God declares this:

> 23. *For all have sinned, and come short of the glory of God;*

— Romans 3:23

What hope is there for us?

Our God is more glorious than those worldly elements of behaviour.

Consider these words from the book of James:

> 17. *But the wisdom that is from above is first pure, then peaceable, gentle, and easy to be intreated, full of mercy and good fruits, without partiality, and without hypocrisy.*
> 18. *And the fruit of righteousness is sown in peace of them that make peace.*
> — James 3:17–18

The Old Testament declares that God will be merciful to us:

> 6. *Seek ye the LORD while he may be found, call ye upon him while he is near:*
> 7. *Let the wicked forsake his way, and the unrighteous man his thoughts: and let him return unto the LORD, and he will have mercy upon him; and to our God, for he will abundantly pardon.*
> — Isaiah 55:6–7

We must never think about acting or thinking in any of those worldly ways again. Make this choice now. Learn to say *"No."* Always step away in haste. It does not hurt.

God has created us with the potential to overcome that side of our human nature. The missing ingredient gets provided when we receive *"the promise of the Father"* which brings the gift of the Holy Spirit.

To receive this wonderful gift from God we need to follow those instructions that Peter gave:

"Repent, and be baptized every one of you in the name of Jesus Christ for the remission of sins, and ye shall receive the gift of the Holy Ghost."

We need to make ourself acceptable through the process of our heart felt repentance to God and Jesus Christ.

An initial image that may come to mind in respect to the term *"Repent"* is that of being utterly sorrowful for something terrible we have done. You could imagine something like this described in the book of Job:

6. *Wherefore I abhor myself, and repent in dust and ashes.*
— Job 42:6

We may have done some terrible things and may need to confront such feelings of complete remorse.

Other people consider themselves as basically *"good people"* and find themselves asking *"Why should I repent?"* *"I haven't done anything wrong."*

Perhaps the thing we have done wrong is that we have turned our back on the God of Creation. This may not get done willfully. What if none of our family or acquaintances are believers and they do not know the truth about the God of the Bible.

We should *"re-think"* our position and our belief (or lack of belief) in God.

Take an honest in-depth look at what the Bible says. We need to read with open eyes, with an open mind and an open heart.

We need to cut out our bad behaviour and replace that with the willingness to get changed from within.

Without the Holy Spirit we are always trying to do everything on our own.

In our own strength we will always fail.

Chapter 3

Our Downfall

The book of Genesis commences with:

> 1. *In the beginning God created the heaven and the earth.*
> — Genesis 1:1

At least six times in Genesis chapter 1, we find God saying, of His Creative work: *"it was good."*

See Genesis chapter 1, and the verses 4, 10, 12, 18, 21 and 25.

When God says *"good"* I expect we could more properly substitute words like brilliant, exceptional, exquisite, extraordinary, magnificent, miraculous, outstanding, remarkable, sensational, splendid, stunning, superb, tremendous, and wonderful and still fall short of the mark.

In the next *"day"* or from the Hebrew *"an unspecified period of time"* we see God creating *"man in our image, after our likeness:"*

> 26. *And God said, Let us make man in our image, after our likeness: and let them have dominion*

over the fish of the sea, and over the fowl of the air, and over the cattle, and over all the earth, and over every creeping thing that creepeth upon the earth.

27. So God created man in his own image, in the image of God created he him; male and female created he them.

28. And God blessed them, and God said unto them, Be fruitful, and multiply, and replenish the earth, and subdue it: and have dominion over the fish of the sea, and over the fowl of the air, and over every living thing that moveth upon the earth.

29. And God said, Behold, I have given you every herb bearing seed, which is upon the face of all the earth, and every tree, in the which is the fruit of a tree yielding seed; to you it shall be for meat.

30. And to every beast of the earth, and to every fowl of the air, and to every thing that creepeth upon the earth, wherein there is life, I have given every green herb for meat: and it was so.

31. And God saw every thing that he had made, and, behold, it was very good. And the evening and the morning were the sixth day.

— Genesis 1:26–31

I have no doubt when God says *"it was very good"* in verse 31, then we will struggle to find superlatives of sufficient meaning and integrity.

We got created in the *"image of God."* We got created in the *likeness* of God.

Can we understand what an exceptional creation God made us to be? The creation of man and woman appear to be the culmination of His entire glorious Creation there. We get created with enormous potential.

God placed Adam and Eve in the garden of Eden; a beautiful

place of His creation:

> 7. *And the LORD God formed man of the dust of the ground, and breathed into his nostrils the breath of life; and man became a living soul.*
> 8. *And the LORD God planted a garden eastward in Eden; and there he put the man whom he had formed.*
> 9. *And out of the ground made the LORD God to grow every tree that is pleasant to the sight, and good for food; the tree of life also in the midst of the garden, and the tree of knowledge of good and evil.*
> — Genesis 2:7–9

The garden contained *"every tree that is pleasant to the sight, and good for food"* and besides these there were two more essentials: *"the tree of life also in the midst of the garden"* and *"the tree of knowledge of good and evil."*

Because God created everything He knows everything there is to know. Almighty God knows the reason why those two particular trees needed to get placed in the garden and He has a reason for their existence there.

God gave the man full responsibility over the care of the garden — *"to dress it and to keep it"* — and He gave him one essential and non-negotiable commandment:

> 15. *And the LORD God took the man, and put him into the garden of Eden to dress it and to keep it.*
> 16. *And the LORD God commanded the man, saying, Of every tree of the garden thou mayest freely eat:*
> 17. *But of the tree of the knowledge of good and evil, thou shalt not eat of it: for in the day that thou eatest thereof thou shalt surely die.*

21

God was there with them when they walked and talked with Him.

There was one life and death condition that Adam chose to break; or couldn't be bothered to keep. I expect you have read the story.

The disappointment of God is evident in the actions He took:

> 22. *And the LORD God said, Behold, the man is become as one of us, to know good and evil: and now, lest he put forth his hand, and take also of the tree of life, and eat, and live for ever:*
> 23. *Therefore the LORD God sent him forth from the garden of Eden, to till the ground from whence he was taken.*
> 24. *So he drove out the man; and he placed at the east of the garden of Eden Cherubims, and a flaming sword which turned every way, to keep the way of the tree of life.*
> — Genesis 3:22–24

Since that time when Adam failed the entrance exam most of the human race remains separated from God.

God is a Spirit, and the conditions are non-negotiable.

God created us with intelligent brains and also the free will to choose to acknowledge Him and to do what He says.

The alternative is for us to turn our back on Him and suffer the consequences. It's our choice.

Almighty God loves us with a love that we can scarce comprehend.

We saw an exposition of God's *'love'* — *'agape'* or *'charity'* — in 1st Corinthians chapter 13, verses 4 to 7.

God wants us to return the same kind of unconditional love towards Him.

He does not want a family of robots, programmed and forced to display an artificial form of affection.

He wants us to be like Him and He has provided a way whereby we can get restored and adopted into His family.

If we are sincere in our approach to God, then it will not be long before we also, will get given the right, to call Him our heavenly Father:

> 14. *For as many as are led by the Spirit of God, they are the sons of God.*
> 15. *For ye have not received the spirit of bondage again to fear; but ye have received the Spirit of adoption, whereby we cry, Abba, Father.*
> — Romans 8:14–15

God does not play games about life and death matters.

We need to take Him at His Word and do everything He commands and recommends that we must needs do.

We need to recognise Almighty God's ultimate authority and give Him all the praise and the glory for the extent of His wonderful creation, both now, and for ever more.

His plan of salvation is everlasting.

Chapter 4

Salvation

God through His Spirit has devised a wonderful plan of Salvation.

God sent His own Son, Jesus Christ, into the world to pay the awful price for our sins and make the way back for us.

Jesus got born with a human body like us. The Bible says He got tempted like us, and yet, He did not sin.

A miraculous change happened to Jesus when He got baptized:

> 16. *And Jesus, when he was baptized, went up straightway out of the water: and, lo, the heavens were opened unto him, and he saw the Spirit of God descending like a dove, and lighting upon him:*
> 17. *And lo a voice from heaven, saying, This is my beloved Son, in whom I am well pleased.*
> — Matthew 3:16–17

Notice that John the Baptist observed: *"the Spirit of God descending like a dove, and lighting upon him."*

This is that key we all need.

The book of John has this to say about where John the Baptist operated:

> 23. *And John also was baptizing in Aenon near to Salim, because there was much water there: and they came, and were baptized.*
> — John 3:23

The important point: *"because there was much water there."*

Baptism involves a complete covering over with the water. This is symbolic of burying our old ungodly — separated from God — life for good.

It's not a token sprinkling when we are babies who are too young to know what the activity means.

Getting baptized is an action we must take when we reach an age of understanding and can know what we are doing.

God does not force us to get baptized. He asks us to do this of our own free will — when we are prepared to have a change of mind or change of thinking and follow His commandments.

In these verses from 1st Peter, chapter 3, we find that our baptism is symbolic of a separation from our old lifestyle. It demonstrates that we have *"a good conscience toward God:"*

> 18. *For Christ also hath once suffered for sins, the just for the unjust, that he might bring us to God, being put to death in the flesh, but quickened by the Spirit:*
> 19. *By which also he went and preached unto the spirits in prison;*
> 20. *Which sometime were disobedient, when once the longsuffering of God waited in the days of*

Noah, while the ark was a preparing, wherein few,
that is, eight souls were saved by water.
21. *The like figure whereunto even baptism doth*
also now save us (not the putting away of the filth
of the flesh, but the answer of a good conscience
toward God,) by the resurrection of Jesus Christ:
22. *Who is gone into heaven, and is on the right*
hand of God; angels and authorities and powers
being made subject unto him.
— 1 Peter 3:18–22

The words in verse 21 say that our baptism in water shows *"the answer of a good conscience toward God."*

Today, if we will agree to remove ourself from our old ways of life, the sin and separation from God, showing our sincerity by getting baptized in water, then Jesus Christ promises that He and the heavenly Father, will come and make their *"abode"* with us:

23. *Jesus answered and said unto him, If a man*
love me, he will keep my words: and my Father
will love him, and we will come unto him, and
make our abode with him.
— John 14:23

Through *"the promise of the Father"* we come full circle and return to life like Adam and Eve enjoyed in the garden of Eden. We now walk and talk with the Spirit of God and with Jesus Christ — every day.

Here is what the book of Romans says:

19. *For as by one man's disobedience many were*
made sinners, so by the obedience of one shall
many be made righteous.
— Romans 5:19

The essential message for us is that although Adam failed the test, God has made another way to enable us to find a way back to be with Him.

Despite knowing what lay before Him, Jesus Christ remained obedient to God's Will. He suffered an awful and agonising death knowing that the heavenly Father, God, promised the result is eternal life.

This miraculous restoration gets made possible because Jesus Christ chose to be obedient to God's will:

> 39. *And he came out, and went, as he was wont, to the mount of Olives; and his disciples also followed him.*
> 40. *And when he was at the place, he said unto them, Pray that ye enter not into temptation.*
> 41. *And he was withdrawn from them about a stone's cast, and kneeled down, and prayed,*
> 42. *Saying, Father, if thou be willing, remove this cup from me: nevertheless not my will, but thine, be done.*
> 43. *And there appeared an angel unto him from heaven, strengthening him.*
> 44. *And being in an agony he prayed more earnestly: and his sweat was as it were great drops of blood falling down to the ground.*
> — Luke 22:39–44

Read verse 42. Remember to say *"Thank you"* to Jesus Christ every day for making that decision for us.

It's difficult for us to understand the perfection of God and the reasons why God's own Son, Jesus Christ, needed to die in our place.

That's an equation I do not yet comprehend.

I expect we will find out one day — when we see Him face to face.

Jesus asked the heavenly Father to forgive us:

> 33. *And when they were come to the place, which is called Calvary, there they crucified him, and the malefactors, one on the right hand, and the other on the left.*
> 34. *Then said Jesus, Father, forgive them; for they know not what they do. And they parted his raiment, and cast lots.*
> — Luke 23:33–34

We give great praise and thanks to Jesus Christ for enduring such torment and we give praises to God for enabling Him to carry that through.

Consider these verses from the gospel of John:

> 7. *Then said Jesus unto them again, Verily, verily, I say unto you, I am the door of the sheep.*
> 8. *All that ever came before me are thieves and robbers: but the sheep did not hear them.*
> 9. *I am the door: by me if any man enter in, he shall be saved, and shall go in and out, and find pasture.*
> 10. *The thief cometh not, but for to steal, and to kill, and to destroy: I am come that they might have life, and that they might have it more abundantly.*
> 11. *I am the good shepherd: the good shepherd giveth his life for the sheep.*
> 12. *But he that is an hireling, and not the shepherd, whose own the sheep are not, seeth the wolf coming, and leaveth the sheep, and fleeth:*

*and the wolf catcheth them, and scattereth the
sheep.*

*13. The hireling fleeth, because he is an hireling,
and careth not for the sheep.*

*14. I am the good shepherd, and know my sheep,
and am known of mine.*

*15. As the Father knoweth me, even so know I the
Father: and I lay down my life for the sheep.*

*16. And other sheep I have, which are not of this
fold: them also I must bring, and they shall hear
my voice; and there shall be one fold, and one
shepherd.*

*17. Therefore doth my Father love me, because I
lay down my life, that I might take it again.*

*18. No man taketh it from me, but I lay it down
of myself. I have power to lay it down, and I have
power to take it again. This commandment have I
received of my Father.*

— John 10:7–18

Verses 14 to 18 explain a lot about what enabled Jesus to do
what He needed to do to secure our salvation.

Jesus trusted in the Father's promise to Him knowing that
He could bring the Father's promise to us.

Look at the promise in verse 10. *"I am come that they might
have life, and that they might have it more abundantly."*

God creates us with the potential to spend eternity with Him
and His Son Jesus Christ.

Think about that. Contemplate the scope of that. Give
praise and thanks to God and to His Son Jesus for the
deliverance of the necessary blessing from above.

On the day of Pentecost we observe that God commenced
pouring out of His Holy Spirit upon all flesh.

Although this is a free gift from God, He does not force His gift on anyone.

God gives us the free will to choose eternal life with Him.

We need to make a humble and repentant approach to God and ask in a circumspect manner for the gift He says He has waiting for us.

In the same way Adam found that God was swift to remove him from the garden of Eden and from the presence of God when he committed the sin of disbelieving God's command — then likewise we need to be mindful of making sure that we keep ourself free from sin.

We know what is right and what is wrong. If ever there is any doubt — please speak with your church pastors and oversight.

Ask first. Not after the event.

God and sin do not mix. The two never co-exist.

We need to receive the miraculous gift of the Holy Spirit and then we never look back to the old and beggarly ways of our prior existence.

Here is a little more of what Paul the apostle wrote in that letter to the Galatians in the chapter before he spoke about those *"fruit of the Spirit"*:

> 4. *But when the fulness of the time was come, God sent forth his Son, made of a woman, made under the law,*
> 5. *To redeem them that were under the law, that we might receive the adoption of sons.*
> 6. *And because ye are sons, God hath sent forth the Spirit of his Son into your hearts, crying, Abba, Father.*
> 7. *Wherefore thou art no more a servant, but a son; and if a son, then an heir of God through Christ.*

8. Howbeit then, when ye knew not God, ye did service unto them which by nature are no gods.
9. But now, after that ye have known God, or rather are known of God, how turn ye again to the weak and beggarly elements, whereunto ye desire again to be in bondage?
— Galatians 4:4–9

Each one of us gets made an *"heir of God through Christ"*.

He exhorts us to whole heartedly refrain from ever turning back *"to the weak and beggarly elements."*

We must take every step possible to prevent from returning to our old lifestyle. This could need us to stop associating with certain people. This could need us to make the effort to change old habits.

Once you receive the promise of the Father you will have a new tool at your command. The small one chapter book of Jude contains these verses:

20. But ye, beloved, building up yourselves on your most holy faith, praying in the Holy Ghost,
21. Keep yourselves in the love of God, looking for the mercy of our Lord Jesus Christ unto eternal life.
— Jude 1:20–21

Verse 20 says we will build up *"ourselves"* whenever we will exercise our faith and *"pray in the Holy Ghost."*

Verse 21 reminds us we are talking about eternal life.

In 1st Corinthians chapter 14, verse 14, Paul the apostle tells us this:

14. For if I pray in an unknown tongue, my spirit prayeth, but my understanding is unfruitful.

— 1 Corinthians 14:14

Who's spirit do we have?

> 12. *Now we have received, not the spirit of the world, but the spirit which is of God; that we might know the things that are freely given to us of God.*
> — 1 Corinthians 2:12

Praying *"in an unknown tongue"* is praying *"in the Holy Ghost."*

Read that again.

We still have responsibility:

> 12. *Blessed is the man that endureth temptation: for when he is tried, he shall receive the crown of life, which the Lord hath promised to them that love him.*
> 13. *Let no man say when he is tempted, I am tempted of God: for God cannot be tempted with evil, neither tempteth he any man:*
> 14. *But every man is tempted, when he is drawn away of his own lust, and enticed.*
> 15. *Then when lust hath conceived, it bringeth forth sin: and sin, when it is finished, bringeth forth death.*
> 16. *Do not err, my beloved brethren.*
> — James 1:12–16

Please read verses 13 and 14 two or three times if needed.

"God cannot be tempted with evil, neither tempteth he any man."

"Every man is tempted, when he is drawn away of his own lust, and enticed."

Remember to say *"No"* without hesitation. Take that responsibility.

If you feel tempted — pray in other tongues asking for help from above.

We need to step away from what we know is wrong and what we know is unacceptable behaviour.

What would you do if Jesus Christ were standing beside you?

Guess what? Both He and God now reside within you by the Holy Spirit. They know your every thought. Your every action.

We have a new hope and a new future. Do not throw that away like Adam. We know better now.

There is nothing better than what awaits those who will adhere to God's will — the ultimate prize is life everlasting.

Chapter 5

Instructions

Initially the outpouring of God's Spirit on all flesh began to take place on the day of Pentecost almost 2,000 years ago.

Many people wonder how an event that took place so long ago can have any bearing on what we do today?

Consider these words of warning, enlightenment and encouragement from the apostle Peter:

> 3. *Knowing this first, that there shall come in the last days scoffers, walking after their own lusts,*
> 4. *And saying, Where is the promise of his coming? for since the fathers fell asleep, all things continue as they were from the beginning of the creation.*
> 5. *For this they willingly are ignorant of, that by the word of God the heavens were of old, and the earth standing out of the water and in the water:*
> 6. *Whereby the world that then was, being overflowed with water, perished:*
> 7. *But the heavens and the earth, which are now, by the same word are kept in store, reserved unto fire against the day of judgment and perdition of*

ungodly men.

8. But, beloved, be not ignorant of this one thing, that one day is with the Lord as a thousand years, and a thousand years as one day.

9. The Lord is not slack concerning his promise, as some men count slackness; but is longsuffering to us-ward, not willing that any should perish, but that all should come to repentance.

10. But the day of the Lord will come as a thief in the night; in the which the heavens shall pass away with a great noise, and the elements shall melt with fervent heat, the earth also and the works that are therein shall be burned up.

11. Seeing then that all these things shall be dissolved, what manner of persons ought ye to be in all holy conversation and godliness,

12. Looking for and hasting unto the coming of the day of God, wherein the heavens being on fire shall be dissolved, and the elements shall melt with fervent heat?

13. Nevertheless we, according to his promise, look for new heavens and a new earth, wherein dwelleth righteousness.

14. Wherefore, beloved, seeing that ye look for such things, be diligent that ye may be found of him in peace, without spot, and blameless.

— 2 Peter 3:3–14

Look at verse 8. God's time scale is different from ours. We need to be aware of factors like that when we get impatient with God. He is not asleep. He knows all things.

Give praise and thanks for the words in verse 9. God is not slack. He is longsuffering towards us *"not willing that any should perish."*

Take notice of the warning in verses 10, 11 and 12.

"What manner of persons ought ye to be in all holy conversation and godliness?"

Take encouragement from what Peter tells us in verses 13 and 14.

We are looking forward to a *"new heavens and a new earth."*

We know when Peter stood up to speak to the gathering crowd and in answer to the question they asked: *"What shall we do?"* he gave everyone these clear instructions:

> 38. *Then Peter said unto them, Repent, and be baptized every one of you in the name of Jesus Christ for the remission of sins, and ye shall receive the gift of the Holy Ghost.*
> 39. *For the promise is unto you, and to your children, and to all that are afar off, even as many as the LORD our God shall call.*
> — Acts 2:38–39

Repent — prepare to get your thinking changed if needed.

We might need to straighten out our lives and actions to conform to the way we know God wants us to be:

> 8. *He hath shewed thee, O man, what is good; and what doth the LORD require of thee, but to do justly, and to love mercy, and to walk humbly with thy God?*
> — Micah 6:8

From my experience, this does not hurt. Try it. We can start to feel good about ourself. Show mercy to others; do not seek revenge. Jesus says we should turn the other cheek, and forgive people who do any wrong to us.

I expect you'll find they do not know about the grace and mercy of God.

Preach the gospel to them in a gentle manner. That could help.

We are God's creation; not the other way around.

Don't shout at God. He can hear you.
Don't curse and swear. He will turn away.

We need to approach God in a circumspect manner with heart felt honesty and humility; a state of repentance where we want to find the truth.

We need to believe what Jesus plainly tells us:

> *"Ye must be born again."*

It's a three step process:

1. **Repent**

Turn aside from doing your own thing all the time.

Make a humble and honest approach towards God.

2. **Get baptized**

Do what God has asked us to do.

Go through the short process of water baptism.

It demonstrates our intentions are good.

It takes a little bit of humility. Yes you'll get wet.

In the church I attend we use warm water.
We have a fresh supply of shorts and tee shirts
and dry towels — for people who don't bring those.

The Bible says *"all have sinned and come short of the glory of God."*

Jesus died to wash away our sins.

3. **Receive God's Holy Spirit**

Ask God for the promise of the Father.

Spend time talking to God with humility and sincerity.

Worship God. Saying the word "*Hallelujah*" gives praise to God and helps to keep us talking.

Say thank you for what you are expecting to receive.

We need to be speaking to let God change the words.

We will know the moment we receive the "*promise of the Father*" because we will start speaking in an unlearned tongue.

If this takes a little while, do not get discouraged.

Ask and keep on asking. Jesus says:

> 7. *Ask, and it shall be given you; seek, and ye shall find; knock, and it shall be opened unto you:*
> 8. *For every one that asketh receiveth; and he that seeketh findeth; and to him that knocketh it shall be opened.*
> — Matthew 7:7–8

Before long we expect there will be a pleasant surprise.

Chapter 6

Walk On In Faith

Having received the infilling of the Holy Ghost, this wonderful gift Jesus called *"the promise of the Father,"* we should then do everything we can to remain strong in the principles of our new found experience in our faith in God and Jesus Christ.

Life can get awkward at times, but in Hebrews 12, we are encouraged to keep looking unto Jesus:

> 1. *Wherefore seeing we also are compassed about with so great a cloud of witnesses, let us lay aside every weight, and the sin which doth so easily beset us, and let us run with patience the race that is set before us,*
> 2. *Looking unto Jesus the author and finisher of our faith; who for the joy that was set before him endured the cross, despising the shame, and is set down at the right hand of the throne of God.*
> 3. *For consider him that endured such contradiction of sinners against himself, lest ye be wearied and faint in your minds.*
> — Hebrews 12:1–3

Why? Because everything is different now. We can choose to take a different approach to life:

> 7. *(For we walk by faith, not by sight:)*
> — 2 Corinthians 5:7

We take no concern for how our life appears. We do not compare ourself to business tycoons, or sporting heroes, or movie stars, or others whom the world may admire.

Rather, we are more concerned with, what God now says about us:

> 26. *For ye are all the children of God by faith in Christ Jesus.*
> — Galatians 3:26

We have become a son or a daughter of the Living God.

If we are His children, then we can expect God to provide great nurture and care for our well-being:

> 19. *But my God shall supply all your need according to his riches in glory by Christ Jesus.*
> — Philippians 4:19

While we may not receive a flashy sports car in response to our request for *"a new set of wheels"* we may find an old bicycle or a skateboard, if one of those is *sufficient* for our *need.*

Understand that God does not promise to supply our every wanton desire. He knows what is best for us. We need to accept that He does.

He would rather we ask for help to *"spread the gospel"* rather than help to *"spread more Jam on our toast."*

Jesus related a parable known as *"The Sower and The Seed"* to help explain to His disciples the relationship between how people hear the instruction in God's Word and how much care they take to guard it and keep to what it says:

> 5. *A sower went out to sow his seed: and as he sowed, some fell by the way side; and it was trodden down, and the fowls of the air devoured it.*
> 6. *And some fell upon a rock; and as soon as it was sprung up, it withered away, because it lacked moisture.*
> 7. *And some fell among thorns; and the thorns sprang up with it, and choked it.*
> 8. *And other fell on good ground, and sprang up, and bare fruit an hundredfold. And when he had said these things, he cried, He that hath ears to hear, let him hear.*
> — Luke 8:5–8

The disciples of Jesus were a little perplexed at what was the underlying meaning of these words:

> 9. *And his disciples asked him, saying, What might this parable be?*
> 10. *And he said, Unto you it is given to know the mysteries of the kingdom of God: but to others in parables; that seeing they might not see, and hearing they might not understand.*
> 11. *Now the parable is this: The seed is the word of God.*
> 12. *Those by the way side are they that hear; then cometh the devil, and taketh away the word out of their hearts, lest they should believe and be saved.*
> 13. *They on the rock are they, which, when they hear, receive the word with joy; and these have no root, which for a while believe, and in time of temptation fall away.*

14. *And that which fell among thorns are they,
which, when they have heard, go forth, and are
choked with cares and riches and pleasures of this
life, and bring no fruit to perfection.*
15. *But that on the good ground are they, which in
an honest and good heart, having heard the word,
keep it, and bring forth fruit with patience.*
— Luke 8:9–15

I hope we want to be like those described in verse 15, who
*"in an honest and good heart, having heard the word, keep it,
and bring forth fruit with patience."*

This means, of course, that we must guard against those
other outcomes described in verses 12, 13 and 14.

People described in verse 12, are those who have the
opportunity to hear the truth of God's Word, but they are
so caught up in their own world that they stop listening to
the truth.

Verse 13 implies that we could — if we do not take care —
soon find ourselves among those which *"for a while believe,
and in time of temptation fall away."*

All kinds of world events and affairs can be tempting to us.
We should take note of what the Bible has to say about
temptation:

13. *There hath no temptation taken you but such
as is common to man: but God is faithful, who
will not suffer you to be tempted above that ye are
able; but will with the temptation also make a way
to escape, that ye may be able to bear it.*
— 1 Corinthians 10:13

Yes we will get *"tempted"* but we do *not* need to *"give in"* to
those temptations. If we keep looking to the Lord, asking for

His guidance, He will help us through those times, so that we can come through un-affected.

If we know an action is wrong say *"No."* Move (*run*) away from the temptation. We will become stronger the next time because we know God is more than able to help us through.

Luke chapter 8, verse 14, describes people who are *"choked with cares and riches and pleasures of this life."* They have too much else going on to be able to devote the time necessary to take care of their new found life in the truth of God's Word. How sad.

When we think about it, what priority should we assign to the attention we give to talking to Almighty God? To singing our praises to Him? To learning more about what He has promised to do? To finding out what God now says of us? And of course, getting involved in the furtherance of the spreading of the gospel, the *"Good News"*?

The Bible warns that the new *"Spirit-filled"* side of us will essentially be at variance with the *"fleshy"* or *"carnal"* side of our old being.

Here we get reminded to *"walk in the Spirit"* and *"be led of the Spirit:"*

> 16. *This I say then, Walk in the Spirit, and ye shall not fulfil the lust of the flesh.*
> 17. *For the flesh lusteth against the Spirit, and the Spirit against the flesh: and these are contrary the one to the other: so that ye cannot do the things that ye would.*
> 18. *But if ye be led of the Spirit, ye are not under the law.*
> — Galatians 5:16–18

Consider this advice from the book of James:

2. My brethren, count it all joy when ye fall into divers temptations;

3. Knowing this, that the trying of your faith worketh patience.

4. But let patience have her perfect work, that ye may be perfect and entire, wanting nothing.

5. If any of you lack wisdom, let him ask of God, that giveth to all men liberally, and upbraideth not; and it shall be given him.

6. But let him ask in faith, nothing wavering. For he that wavereth is like a wave of the sea driven with the wind and tossed.

7. For let not that man think that he shall receive any thing of the Lord.

8. A double minded man is unstable in all his ways.

— James 1:2–8

We may at times experience what seems to be a *"trying of our faith."*

What are we to do? Talk to God. Look at verses 5 and 6.

God is a Spirit. We must pray in other tongues.

James chapter 1, verse 6 says *"ask in faith, nothing wavering."*

Believe that God, Who has filled us with the Holy Spirit, has unlimited ability. We read that for Him *"nothing shall be impossible:"*

37. For with God nothing shall be impossible.
— Luke 1:37

In James chapter 1, verse 3 (above), it tells us that the *"trying of your faith"* when we find ourselves wondering and even being doubtful can be good for us because this will help to increase our patience.

We will still need to have a good supply of (i.e., command of our own) patience at times throughout our lives.

We need to remember that God, having filled us with the Holy Spirit, will not let us fail.

We keep looking to Him, and praying to Him, with the new capability we have — *'speaking in other tongues'*.

Make the decision to get to as many church meetings as you can.

If you attend with a prayerful attitude of listening for and hoping for more information to help you with your walk in the Lord then I know God can fulfil that desire.

Well meaning family and friends could attempt to persuade you to stay away when there is a clash between family events and church meetings.

That can get awkward at first. Let family and friends know that you have a new schedule now and your new found experience with the Living God will take priority. Sorry. Can that get rescheduled for earlier or later in the day?

Show them you are certain of your faith. Tell them why. You have received a gift from God and you know that because you can speak in other tongues.

Tell them how good life has become. One day they might come along to see for themselves.

If they love you and respect you as a person they will support your decisions to worship God first. There is nothing more important than our spiritual welfare:

25. *Not forsaking the assembling of ourselves together, as the manner of some is; but exhorting*

*one another: and so much the more, as ye see the
day approaching.*
— Hebrews 10:25

People may think we are heartless. Jesus did not think so.
Go back and read the parable of the Sower and the Seed.

Jesus also made statements like these:

> 35. *For I am come to set a man at variance
> against his father, and the daughter against her
> mother, and the daughter in law against her
> mother in law.*
> 36. *And a man's foes shall be they of his own
> household.*
> 37. *He that loveth father or mother more than me
> is not worthy of me: and he that loveth son or
> daughter more than me is not worthy of me.*
> — Matthew 10:35–37

When He was calling His disciples and followers He said:

> 59. *And he said unto another, Follow me. But
> he said, Lord, suffer me first to go and bury my
> father.*
> 60. *Jesus said unto him, Let the dead bury their
> dead: but go thou and preach the kingdom of God.*
> 61. *And another also said, Lord, I will follow thee;
> but let me first go bid them farewell, which are at
> home at my house.*
> 62. *And Jesus said unto him, No man, having put
> his hand to the plough, and looking back, is fit for
> the kingdom of God.*
> — Luke 9:59–62

We do not return to our old lifestyle. If you are like me that
life was going in the wrong direction. God has brought us
into His family now.

Yes, we still love our natural family and good friends. If we love them we will preach the gospel first. They may not hear what we say — yet.

Invite them to a church meeting. Be patient with them.

I know God was (and is) patient with me. Do not always try to push the boundaries at both ends of the scale.

We need to spend quality time giving praise and worship to God. Church meetings is an important part of that. There is a lot to learn. There is a lot for which we give God thanks.

Chapter 7

Fruit of The Spirit

As a way to help me keep those nine *"fruit of the Spirit"* upper-most in my mind I wrote a little piece of music to help me remember their names.

In recent times I have turned to using a clever and most capable music notation system called: *"Lilypond."*

Please visit their web page for more details:

```
https://lilypond.org
```

LilyPond is free software and part of the GNU Project. It's published under the GNU General Public License.

The Lilypond system will run on Linux or Windows or Apple PCs and there is a GUI front end called "frescobaldi" to help make text input and music output easier.

I happen to use the Linux system because I have worked with this for decades. It is my computer system of choice.

Unlike expensive graphical score editing systems, Lilypond presents a compiled symbolic language system that uses a plain text file describing the music elements.

The note names, note pitch, note duration and other music articulation information gets defined with the use of plain text characters and numbers and symbols.

It's not as difficult as that may sound. If you use a computer and can find a plain text editor program (not a word processor application) then you are set to go after you find and install the Lilypond software.

When initially installed the Lilypond system uses lower-case letters 'a' through 'g' for the note names and uses the addition of 'es' to flatten a note, or 'is' to sharpen a note. For example: 'ees' is a flattened E note, and 'fis' is a sharpened F note.

Although I do not sight read music (the dots and squiggles on a page), I knew where to find the notes I wanted on the fret board of my guitar.

I began to pick those out, slowly, letting my ear discern the note pitches I wanted and writing down the note names as I went.

Next I needed to determine the note lengths in the 8/8 timing I had chosen. It was a slow process at first.

In Lilypond we can use either *absolute* pitch or *relative* note pitch. I prefer to use *absolute* note pitch. I know, I am a bit weird.

After a single or three-character note name, we can append one or more right single quote (') characters to *raise* the note by an *octave*. Or we can add one or more comma (,) characters to *lower* the note by an *octave*.

The duration for a note gets specified by appending a small integer, like '2' for a half note (a *minim*), '4' for a quarter note (a *crotchet*), '8' for an eighth note (a *quaver*), or '16' for a sixteenth note (a *semi-quaver*), etc.

A dotted note gets indicated with one or more dot ('.')

characters appended after that.

For example writing the three characters:

```
d4.
```

defines a 'd' note to get sounded as a dotted quarter note.

The second and subsequent notes of a sequence of notes of *equal* length do not need a duration number until that note length needs to change. For example:

```
d'4 d'8 d' d' c' b4
```

This produces a *quarter* note, four *eighth* notes, and another *quarter* note. One bar in my 8/8 music.

An anacrusis or pickup or partial measure can get written with code like this:

```
\partial 4 b8 c'8 |
```

The vertical bar character ('|') at the end of that represents a bar line.

A rest (the absence of sound) gets specified by the letter 'r' with a duration number appended.

A tuplet of notes, for example, five notes played in the time of four, gets written like this:

```
\times 4/5 { d'8 e'8 fis'8 g'8 a'8 }
```

Other music elements like the *"tie"* or the *"slur"* get specified with a tilde (~) character between two notes that need to get tied to produce a longer duration:

```
e'4~ e'8
```

A pair of parentheses '(' and ')' characters get used to show a "*slur*" across two or more notes of different pitch:

```
b8( c'8)
```

There is other notation markup such as '<' and '>' to enclose the notes of a chord:

```
< c e g >4
```

Where you see pairs of angle brackets like '<<' and '>>' these enclose parallel sections of music using separate staves or clefs.

You can select the appropriate Clef for your music with entries like:

```
\clef "treble"  \clef "bass"
```

Other clefs include:

```
\clef "tenor"  \clef "treble_8"
```

Specify the Time Signature with:

```
\time 3/4  \time 4/4  \time 8/8
```

Set the Key for a piece with:

```
\key g \major  \key a \minor
```

The Lilypond markup language permits the user to define *variables* for reuse within a piece of music:

```
var = { ... }
```

and down further we can use:

```
\var \var
```

to sound and repeat the music that got defined between the two curly brace characters '{' and '}'.

There are elements to define a '\scrore { ... }' and the score *layout* with '\layout { ... }' and there is a request to produce MIDI output with '\midi { }' and other items like headings and lyrics.

The percent character ('%') commences a line of comment text.

Here is the Lilypond source file I produced to help me determine the melody for my song:

```
1   %
2   % Program:
3   %    frots.ly --> "Fruit of The Spirit"
4   %
5   % Author:
6   %    Lawson Hanson, 20220522.
7   %
8   % Purpose:
9   %    Lilypond melody and lyrics
10  %
11  \version "2.20.0"
12
13  #(set-default-paper-size "a4")
14  #(set-global-staff-size 24 )
```

```
15
16   \header {
17       title = "Fruit of The Spirit"
18       composer = "Lawson Hanson"
19       arranger = \markup { "22-May-2022" }
20       meter = "andante" %%% "walking pace"
21       tagline = #ff
22       copyright = "Copyright (C) Lawson I. Hanson 2022.
23                             All rights reserved."
24   }
25
26   lineOne = {
27       \partial 4 b8   c'8 |
28       %%            Now   the
29         d'4     d'8  d'8  d'8     c'8  b4 |
30       %% fruit  of   the  Spi -- rit  is,
31
32         d'4   e'4   d'4
33       %% Love, Joy, Peace,
34
35         b8(  c'8) |
36       %% Long --
37         d'8     d'8     d'4
38       %% suf -- fer -- ing,
39
40         d'8     e'8     d'8    c'8 |
41       %% Gen -- tle -- ness   and
42         b4        a4 r4
43       %% Good -- ness,
44
45     e'4 ~ | e'8
46       %% Faith,
47         fis'8    fis'8 r8 fis'8   g'8 r8 a'8 |
48       %% Meek -- ness       and    Tem -- per --
49         g'4.    r4.
50       %% ance.
51   }
52
53   theMelody = {
```

```
54        \clef treble
55        \key g \major
56        \time 8/8
57        \tempo 8 = 180
58
59        \lineOne
60    }
61
62    theLyrics = \lyricmode {
63        Now the fruit of the Spi -- rit is,
64        Love, Joy, Peace,
65        Long -- suff -- er -- ing,
66        Gen -- tle -- ness and Good -- ness,
67        Faith, Meek -- ness and Tem -- per -- ance.
68    }
69
70    \score {
71        <<
72            \new Voice = "one" { \autoBeamOff \theMelody }
73            \new Lyrics \lyricsto "one" \theLyrics
74        >>
75        \layout { }
76        \midi { }
77    }
78
```

When I run the following Linux shell command:

```
$ lilypond frots.ly
```

The dollar symbol ($) at the start of the line represents my shell prompt. Do not enter that character.

The 'lilypond' command compiles the plain text file named 'frots.ly' and provided there are no errors in my code I will get two new output files:

```
frots.midi
```

and:

```
frots.pdf
```

The PDF file is a printable form of the music. On Linux I use the 'qpdfview' program to display the PDF file:

```
$ qpdfview frots.pdf
```

To listen to the music, the MIDI file can get sent to a MIDI player. On Linux I use the 'timidity' program:

```
$ timidity frots.midi
```

Lilypond Guitar Notes

Here is a list of Lilypond absolute note names for a six string guitar in a standard tuning:

```
1    #
2    # Program:
3    #    gtr-lyp-notes.txt
4    #
5    # Author:
6    #    Lawson Hanson, 20211103.
7    #
8    # Purpose:
9    #    Lilypond absolute note names for a
10   #    six-string guitar in standard tuning:
11   #
12   # Format:
13   # ------
14   #    Fret   String numbers -->
15   #    -1     6      5      4      3      2      1
```

```
16  #   0    e,    a,    d    g    b     e'
17  #   1    f,    ais,  dis  gis  c'    f'
18  #   ...
19  #   12   e,    a,    d    g    b'    e'
20  #   ...
21  #   19   b     e'    a'   d''  fis'' b''
22  #
23  # Notes (fret representations):
24  #   1. Fret '-1' the string numbers line
25  #   2. Fret '0'  the Nut (an open string)
26  #
27  -1  6    5     4     3    2    1
28  0   e,   a,    d     g    b    e'
29      ========================================
30  1   f,   ais,  dis   gis  c'   f'
31  2   fis, b,    e     a    cis' fis'
32  3   g,   c     f     ais  d'   g'
33      ----------------------------------------
34  4   gis, cis   fis   b    dis' gis'
35  5   a,   d     g     c'   e'   a'
36      ----------------------------------------
37  6   ais, dis   gis   cis' f'   ais'
38  7   b,   e     a     d'   fis' b'
39      ----------------------------------------
40  8   c    f     ais   dis' g'   c''
41  9   cis  fis   b     e'   gis' cis''
42  10  d    g     c'    f'   a'   d''
43      ----------------------------------------
44  11  dis  gis   cis'  fis' ais' dis''
45  12  e    a     d'    g'   b'   e''
46      ----------------------------------------
47  13  f    ais   dis'  gis' c''  f''
48  14  fis  b     e'    a'   cis'' fis''
49  15  g    c'    f'    ais' d''  g''
50  16  gis  cis'  fis'  b    dis'' gis''
51  17  a    d'    g'    c''  e''  a''
52  18  ais  dis'  gis'  cis'' f'' ais''
53  19  b    e'    a'    d''  fis'' b''
54  20  c'   f'    ais'  dis'' g'' c'''
```

59

I find that helpful when I am trying to figure out the note name information for the notes at the fret stops I am playing.

Lilypond includes exceptionally good documentation, all available at the extensive resources found on the web page I listed near the start of this chapter.

There is introductory material with tutorials as well as more in-depth learning and reference material.

Here is the resulting musical score for my song produced by running the 'lilypond' command to compile the plain text source file listed earlier above:

Fruit of The Spirit

Lawson Hanson
22-May-2022

andante

Now the fruit of the Spi-rit is, Love, Joy, Peace, Long -

suffering, Gentleness and Goodness, Faith, Meekness and Temperance.

Copyright (C) Lawson I. Hanson 2022.   All rights reserved.

Chapter 8

More Music

In my younger days I played in a small band at the church I
have attended for almost 50 years.

```
https://www.revivalcentres.org
```

Age and health issues have slowed me down, yet there are
some examples of my music on-line.

To listen to this music you could try a YouTube™ search:

```
https://www.YouTube.com/results?search_query=Lawson+Hanson+music
```

You should find a *"Remixed: Lord God Almighty,"* and other
songs like: *"Faith," "He Is Lord," "On A Day Like This"* and
"Prodigal Son."

Note: You can find sixteen (16) different songs. Each
YouTube *track* has a single *still* image, not a video clip
(other than the advertising they seem to display — please
hit "Skip"), and each should be playable on a low bandwidth
connection; i.e., will not use too much of your Internet data
limit.

In an undirected Google™ search, you may need to use quotation marks around my two names because there are other people called *"Lawson,"* and a band named *"Hanson,"* none of whom are the same *"Lawson Hanson"* who resides in my skin.

Otherwise, there are two *Albums,* each of which has eight tracks. I have distributed these through DistroKid™and people should be able to find the tracks through digital download and/or audio streaming channels such as: Amazon™, Apple Music™, Spotify™and perhaps some others. An example of these located at Apple Music is:

- He Is Lord

  https://music.apple.com/au/album/he-is-lord/1473958665

- Prodigal Son's Return

  https://music.apple.com/au/album/prodigal-sons-return/1473966231

Or on Spotify:

- He Is Lord

  https://open.spotify.com/album/6TC5awGoyok3cXY7fU9tkl

- Prodigal Son's Return

  https://open.spotify.com/album/5RuDTHcTKAzYYoKHBeO5Os

Accreditations

Over the course of more than four decades I have performed my music live with the accompaniment of different musicians.

I offer my sincere thanks and great appreciation to the talented individuals who spent countless hours of their precious time in rehearsals and preparations for the performances we managed to present.

We made rough recordings of the music over the years. Accompanying my own lyrics, melodies, vocals and rhythm guitar, the recordings variously include other instrumental and vocal performances by:

By Musical Instrument

- Bass Guitar:

    - Bradley Parker-Hill
    - Mark Stanborough

- Drums:

    - Jonathon Longfield
    - Mark Stanborough
    - Nigel Picknell
    - Paul Anastassopoulos
    - Stuart Bowden

- Lead Guitar:

    - Clive Smith
    - Mark Stanborough

- Saxophone:

- Mark Stanborough
  - Peter deMunk

- Sound Recording:

  - Mark Stanborough

- Vocals:

  - Paul Anastassopoulos
  - Peter deMunk

By the same author

Nonfiction

Epub

Glory to God Everywhere You Are There
Describes the origins of my simple song of praise
2025, ISBN 9781764057820
.

Jesus Says You Must Be Born Again
The most important information the world affords
2025, ISBN 9781764057813

Nonfiction

Paperback

Glory to God Everywhere You Are There
Describes the origins of my simple song of praise
2025, ISBN 9781764057837
.

Jesus Says You Must Be Born Again
The most important information the world affords
2025, ISBN 9781764057806
.

Paul's Question
Have you received the Holy Spirit?
2023, ISBN 9798857128381

.

Linux Bread Crumbs
Learn to use Linux
2023, ISBN 9798364005830

.

To Day If You Will Hear His Voice
Believe in God
2022, ISBN 9798831130669

.

Take Another Look
Please take another look
2022, ISBN 9798437605554

.

Song Lyrics
Notes and lyrics for 16 of my songs
2022, ISBN 9798434494120

Fiction

Paperback

The Ravenscroft Algorithm
Fictitious cyber crime
2022, ISBN 9798842106202

.

Broke Reef
Fictitious shipwreck on a W.Aust. Reef
2022, ISBN 9798428316940

www.ingramcontent.com/pod-product-compliance
Lightning Source LLC
Chambersburg PA
CBHW060535030426
42337CB00021B/4271